OSHO

T0002570

the Colors of Your Life

- Meditative & Transformative Coloring Book -

OSHO MEDIA INTERNATIONAL
New York · Zurich · Mumbai
an imprint of OSHO INTERNATIONAL
www.osho.com/oshointernational

Distributed by Publishers Group Worldwide, www.pgw.com

Printed in USA by Bang Printing

ISBN 978-1-938755-41-5

CREATIVITY

Become a child again and you will be creative.
All children are creative. Creativity needs freedom – freedom from the mind, freedom
from knowledge, freedom from prejudices. A creative person is one who can try the
new. A creative person is not a robopath. Robopaths are never creative, they are
repetitive. So become a child again.

Creativity has nothing to do with any activity in particular: with painting, poetry,
dancing, singing. It has nothing to do with anything in particular.
Anything can be creative – you bring that quality to the activity. Activity itself is
neither creative nor uncreative: you can paint in an uncreative way; you can sing in an
uncreative way; you can clean the floor in a creative way, you can cook in a creative way.
Creativity is the quality that you bring to the activity you are doing. It is an attitude, an
inner approach – how you look at things.
So the first thing to be remembered: don't confine creativity to anything in particular.
A man is creative, and if he is creative whatsoever he does, even if he walks, you can see
in his walking there is creativity. Even if he sits silently and does nothing, even non-
doing will be a creative act. Buddha sitting under the bodhi tree doing nothing is the
greatest creator the world has ever known.
Once you understand it – that it is you, the person who is creative or uncreative – then
this problem disappears.
Not everybody can be a painter, and there is no need also. If everybody is a painter, the
world will be very ugly; it will be difficult to live. And not everybody can be a dancer,
and there is no need. But everybody can be creative.
Whatsoever you do, if you do it joyfully, if you do it lovingly, if your act of doing
it is not purely economical, then it is creative. If you have something growing out of it
within you, if it gives you growth, it is spiritual, it is creative, it is divine...
Love what you do. Be meditative while you are doing it, whatsoever it is – irrelevant of
the fact of what it is.

Creativity means loving whatsoever you do — enjoying, celebrating it, as a gift of existence! Maybe nobody comes to know about it... If your act is your love affair, then it becomes creative. Small things become great by the touch of love and delight.

To be and to be creative are synonymous. It is impossible to be and not to be creative... Our whole attitude about life is money oriented. And money is one of the most uncreative things one can become interested in. Our whole approach is power oriented, and power is destructive, not creative. A man who is after money will become destructive because money has to be robbed, exploited. It has to be taken away from many people, only then can you have it. Power simply means you have to make many people impotent, you have to destroy them — only then will you be powerful, can you be powerful. Remember that these are destructive acts.

A creative act enhances the beauty of the world. It gives something to the world, it never takes anything from it. A creative person comes into the world, enhances the beauty of the world — a song here, a painting there. He makes the world dance better, enjoy better, love better, meditate better. When he leaves this world, he leaves a better world behind him. Nobody may know him, somebody may know him — that is not the point. But he leaves the world a better world, tremendously fulfilled because his life has been of some intrinsic value...

Be a giver. Share whatsoever you can. And remember, I am not making any distinction between small things and great things. If you can smile whole-heartedly, hold somebody's hand and smile, then it is a creative act, a great creative act. Just embrace somebody to your heart and you are creative. Just look with loving eyes at somebody; just a loving look can change the whole world of a person.

Be creative. Don't be worried about what you are doing. One has to do many things, but do everything creatively, with devotion. Then your work becomes worship. Then whatsoever you do is prayer. And whatsoever you do is an offering at the altar.

~ Osho

CELEBRATION

The workaholics have done immense harm to the world. And the greatest harm they have done is that they have deprived life of its moments of celebration and festivity. It is because of them that there is so little festivity in the world, and every day it is becoming more and more dull and dreary and miserable. In fact, entertainment has taken the place of celebration in the present world. But entertainment is quite different from celebration; entertainment and celebration are never the same. In celebration you are a participant; in entertainment you are only a spectator. In entertainment you watch others playing for you. So while celebration is active, entertainment is passive. In celebration you dance, while in entertainment you watch someone dancing, for which you pay him. In this world of consciousness, nothing is as helpful as celebration.

THE FOOL

"The Fool" in the Tarot cards...Th
Fool is standing on the cliff, one
foot dangling, hanging over the
cliff – and he is not aware, and
he is looking at the stars and he
is very happy. His head must be
full of dreams.

A little foolishness and a little
wisdom is good, and the right
combination makes you a
buddha – a little foolishness
and a little wisdom. Don't be just
wise or else you will be a long
face; don't be just a fool or else
you will become suicidal. A little
foolishness, enough to enjoy life,
and a little wisdom to avoid the
errors, that will do.

EXISTENCE

You are going through a transformation.

You have lived your life horizontally, concerned with the trivia of day-to-day life.

In meditation your horizontal line becomes a vertical line. When you are vertical you start moving upwards — more and more blossoms come and you start also simultaneously growing in depth — almost as deep as the Pacific Ocean.

Growing upwards and downwards simultaneously is the only miracle I know of, because this miracle makes you part of eternity. You are no longer mortal, immortality is your home.

The whole existence is your home. The cosmos, infinite and eternal, is your ultimate home.

THE CREATOR

We only live in moments when we are creative. When we create something, that is the only living moment. It doesn't matter what is being created, the feeling that you have created something is the only thing. You have become a creator. The moment you feel that you have become a creator – maybe just a toy, just a painting, just a piece of poetry or anything else – the moment you feel that you have become a creator, something is fulfilled in you, and something begins to flower.

INNER VOICE

At the innermost center of our being is immense light, immense clarity. But we live on the periphery where everything is noisy.

Meditation is the art of hearing our own inner voice. It is there, it is always there. Your being always wants to talk to you. It has many messages to give to you; in each situation it immediately gives you a message. And it is always right; there is no question of right and wrong, there is no question of choice. The being simply shows you what to do, where to move, in what direction. It is clear-cut; there are no ifs and buts. And the clarity is so profound that you cannot miss it; you will be able to see the light.

CREATIVITY

Learn to lead a creative life.
Creativity means that you do
something solely for the joy it
gives you. You can sculpt, write
a song, sing a song, play the
sitar – it does not matter what
you do, but do it only for
pleasure and not as
a profession. Do something
in life which is only for
pleasure, something which is
not your profession. Then all
the destructive energy will be
transformed and will
become creative.

THE REBEL

How is it that all educational institutions in the world teach you to be imitators and they never ask you to be yourself? The most important reason is that if everyone becomes himself, he will be a free individual, a rebel — not a conformist, a camp follower. He will be a danger to the institutions of parents, teachers, priests, managers of society, and to society itself. Every society is afraid of non-conformists and rebels. It honors the conformists, the yes-sayers. That is why everybody, from the president down to the parents pressures children, with one voice, to be followers, imitators. Otherwise they can't be certain who will turn into what.

THE LOVERS

Even in love, when you think you are together, you are not together. There are two alonenesses. In real love nothing is lost. When two lovers are sitting – if they are really lovers and they don't try to possess each other and they don't try to dominate each other... because that is not love; that is the way of hatred, the way of violence. If they love and if the love is coming out of their aloneness, you will see two beautiful alonenesses together. They are like two Himalayan peaks, high in the sky, but separate. They don't interfere. In fact deep love only reveals your pure aloneness to you.

AWARENESS

Listen. Just close your eyes and listen. Listen quietly, in silence. Listen to the chirping of the birds, to the gusts of the winds swaying the trees, to the cry of a child, to the sound of the water wheel at the well. Simply listen, to the movement of the breath and to your heartbeat.
A new kind of peace and serenity will descend upon you. You will find that although there is noise outside there is silence inside. You will find you have entered a new dimension of peace. Then, there are no thoughts, only pure consciousness remains. And in this medium of emptiness your attention, your awareness turns toward the place that is your real abode. From the outside you turn toward your home.

COURAGE

Fear and courage, both
destroy – but fear simply
destroys. The seed simply goes
rotten. When you sow the seed
of courage in the soil, then too it
dies – but it doesn't go rotten.
It dies...it dies
into a new phenomenon.
A sprout comes up.
Courage will kill you as much
as fear, but fear will simply kill
you without giving you a
new life. Courage will give you
a new life. Choose courage –
always choose courage.

ALONENESS

You can be alone, but that aloneness may not be true aloneness. It may be only loneliness, and you may be thinking and fantasizing about all kinds of things.
Aloneness comes out of awareness; it has nothing to do with where you are in the outside world but where you are in the inside world.

CHANGE

The world, the creation, is in
constant change, but nothing
can be created or destroyed.
Change is the reality. By change
I mean that only the form
changes, never the substance. The
basic remains always the same;
only the mode of expression, the
form, changes. And this change
is continuous; it is eternal.

BREAKTHROUGH

Modern researchers, particularly dream researchers, have stumbled upon a new kind of dream just recently; they call it the breakthrough dream. This is a breakthrough dream...

A breakthrough dream is a dream in which some kind of awareness arises in you. The ordinary dream is unconscious, passive: you simply go on watching, no awareness arises in you, you are simply identified with the dream...he breakthrough dream is different: it is not passive, it is active; it is not just possessing you, you remain in some way alert in it.

NEW VISION

A dream is yours.
A vision is not yours.
A dream is yours: you were
imagining, you created it,
it was your fantasy.
A vision is something out of the
blue that you have never thought
about, not even a part of it has
ever been thought by you. It is so
utterly new — then it is a vision.
A vision is from existence, a
dream is from your mind.
If unimaginable, it must
be bliss itself.

TRANSFORMATION

Ready-made answers don't help. Unless you discover the answer yourself, unless the truth is your own experience, you are not going to have a transformation. Information is not transformation. You can become very knowledgeable through information, but your ignorance remains the same. The greatest knowledgeable person is ignorant, is just like any ignorant person who knows nothing.

INTEGRATION

Integration has nothing to do
with "becoming."
In fact, all efforts to become brin[g]
disintegration.
Integration is already there at th[e]
deepest core of your being;
it has not to be brought in.
At your very center you are
integrated, otherwise you could
not exist at all...
You are alive, you are breathing
you are conscious; life is moving
so there must be a hub to the
wheel of life. You may not be
aware, but it is there. Without i[t]
you cannot be.

CONDITIONING

Individuality is given by existence; personality is imposed by the society. Personality is social convenience. Society cannot tolerate individuality, because individuality will not follow like a sheep. Individuality has the quality of the lion; the lion moves alone.

The sheep are always in the crowd, hoping that being in the crowd will feel cozy. Being in the crowd one feels more protected, secure. If somebody attacks, there is every possibility in a crowd to save yourself — but alone?

Only the lions move alone. And every one of you is born a lion, but the society goes on conditioning you, programming your mind as a sheep.

THUNDERBOL͡

It is a sudden experience, no
preparation, no rehearsal,
no discipline, no path. Suddenl͡
you open your eyes as if a
thunderbolt has hit you and
the sleep of millions of years is
broken. In that awakening you
know the mystery of existence.

SILENCE

The art of life begins with meditation. And by meditation I mean silence of the mind, silence of the heart, reaching to the very center of your being and finding the treasure that is your reality. Once you have known it, you can radiate love, you can radiate life, you can radiate creativity. Your words will become poetic, your gestures will have grace; even your silence will have a song to it.

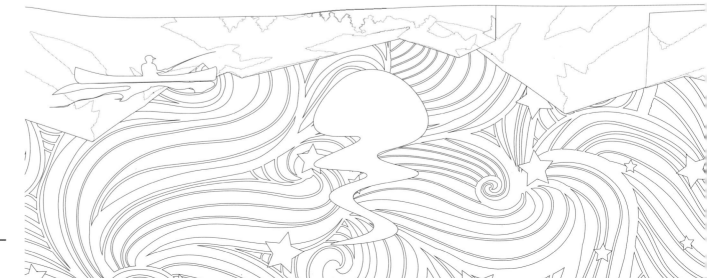

PAST LIVES

Why should you be interested in
past life"? It is finished, it is gon
it is no more! It has no existence
anywhere, no validity.
It is possible that a man may
have been an animal or a bird
in his past life. What we need
to be aware of, though, is not to
continue to be a bird or a beast
in this life.

INNOCENCE

Only a meditator comes
of age; for the first time he
becomes mature, grown-up. All
childishness disappears
from him.
And the beauty is, when all
childishness disappears from
you, you again become childlike
but on a different plane. No
childishness but absolutely
childlike – the same purity,
the same innocence, the same
wonder, the same awe. Again
existence becomes a mystery.

BEYOND ILLUSION

The mind is a kind of illusion. It does not allow you to see the reality as it is; it distorts it. It gives its own color to it. It projects its desires on it. It uses reality as a screen. It does not give you a clear picture of what the case is. ...To see reality one has to put the mind aside; one has to learn to see reality without the mind interfering. And that's what meditation is all about: a methodology to put the mind aside... even for a few moments.

COMPLETION

No question is ever complete, because the completion of a question will mean it has its answer in itself. A question by its very nature is incomplete. It is a desire, a longing, an inquiry, because something needs to be completed. It is part of human consciousness that it demands completion. Leave anything incomplete and it becomes an obsession; complete it and you are free of it. Completion brings freedom.

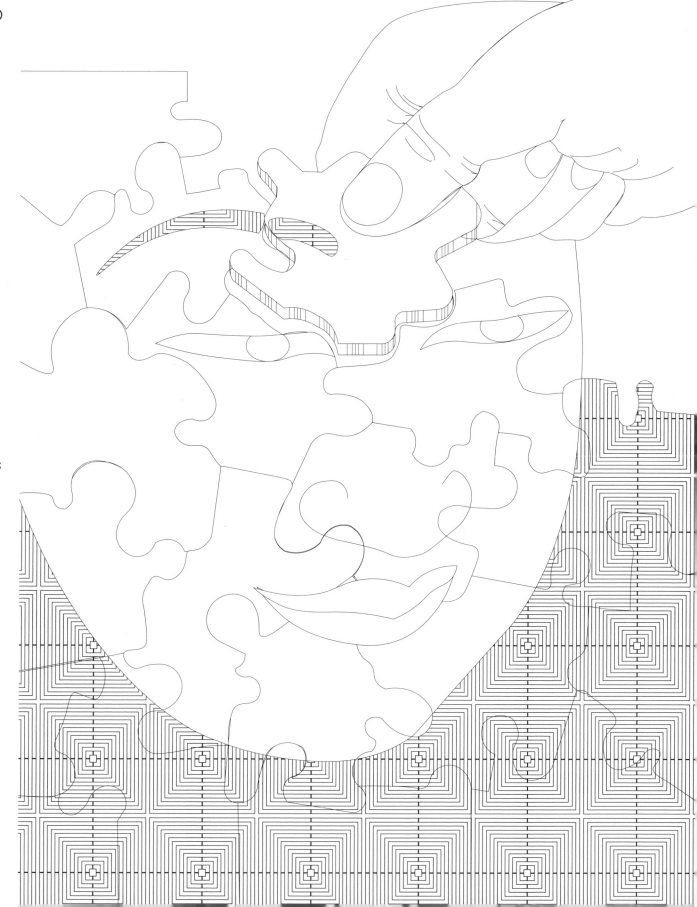

THE MASTER

Without being a master of
oneself, your life is empty, vain,
meaningless. It can't have any
poetry, it can't have any joy,
it can't have any ecstasy. And
ecstasy, joy, is your birthright —
but you can have it only when
you attain to this worth,
to this worthiness.

Become aware, trust, start seeing
— drop all beliefs and all doubts,
and the goal is not far away. You
need not go anywhere. If you can
trust, meditate, see, if you can
awaken to the eternal law, you
are the master — not the master
of anybody else but the master of
yourself. And that is
the true mastery.

INTENSITY

Each moment, whatever you are doing, do it with full awareness, with totality, intensity, love; and do it as if it is the greatest thing in the world to do. Make it an art, so that each moment of your life becomes the life of an artist.

PLAYFULNESS

The whole human mind has
been trained to be a worker.
That's why duty has been praised
and playfulness condemned,
business praised and gambling
condemned – because
a gambler is playful and
a businessman is serious. The
businessman is respected; a
gambler is simply condemned...
I am just emphasizing the quality
of playfulness, the quality that
can enjoy and be and is not
worried about results.

HEALING

The word "meditation" and the word "medicine" come from the same root. Medicine means that which heals the physical, and meditation means that which heals the spiritual. Both are healing powers.

RECEPTIVITY

Receptivity is a state of no-mind. In the mind, you are miles away from being. The more you think, the less you are. The less you think, the more you are. Receptivity simply means dropping the garbage that you go on carrying in your head. And much garbage is there, utterly useless. The mind means the past. Now the past is no more of any use; it has happened, and it is never going to happen again, because in reality nothing ever repeats.

TRUST

Trust life — there is no need of any other trust. Trust life and it leads you spontaneously and naturally to the ultimate, the truth, God — or whatsoever you want to name it.

The river of life is flowing towards the ocean. If you trust, you flow in the river. You are already in the river, but you are clinging to some dead roots on the bank, or you are trying to fight against the current. Clinging to scriptures, clinging to dogmas, doctrines, is not allowing the river to take you with her. Drop all doctrines, all dogmas, all scriptures. Life is the only scripture, the only bible. Trust it and allow it to take you to the ocean, to the ultimate.

UNDERSTANDING

A bird on the wing and the same
bird in the cage are not the same
at all. The bird in the cage is no
more the same because it has
lost its freedom, it has lost its
tremendous sky. It has lost
the joy of dancing in the wind,
in the rain, in the sun. You may
have given it a golden cage but
you have destroyed its dignity, it
freedom, its joy.

CONTROL

Control has become such a
supreme value. It is not a value
at all. A controlled person is a
dead person; a controlled person
is not necessarily a disciplined
person. Discipline is totally
different. Discipline comes out of
awareness; control comes
out of fear.

MORALITY

My definition of morality is
different than any definition that
has ever been given.
My definition is: whatever you
do out of your meditation is
moral. And whatever you do in
your spiritual sleep, unaware, is
immoral. It may look moral to
other people. But I will not say
it is moral unless your action
comes out of awareness — and
awareness is a by-product
of meditation.

FIGHTING

Life has immense treasures, which remain unknown to people because they don't have time. Their whole time is engaged in some kind of fight with someone – the other. The other contains the whole world. And the greatest calamity that happens is that when you are fighting with the other, you slowly, slowly forget yourself. Your whole focus becomes the other, and when the focus becomes the other, you are lost. Then when are you going to remember yourself?

MIND

Mind is simply a collection of
memories of the past, and — out
of those memories — imagination
about the future.
Mind does not know three tenses
It knows only two: past
and future.
Present is nonexistential to
the mind. The existential is
nonexistential to the mind; and
the nonexistentials are existential
to the mind.
How to be in the present? — that
is the whole knack of meditation

ABUNDANCE

It is natural to be selfish. And the miracle is, if you are really selfish, out of your selfishness there will be so much abundance of intelligence, love, respect, that you are bound to share it with others. Because the economics of the inner world is: the more you share, the more you have. Naturally, you want to share it more and more. Why not to the whole world?

A small human heart is capable of filling the whole universe with love. But first it has to learn the art; and you have to begin with yourself.

FLOWERING

Just be yourself, utterly yourself.
And don't be bothered what kind
of flower you turn out to be.
It does not matter whether
you are a rose or a lotus or a
marigold. It does not matter.
What matters is flowering. Let
me repeat: the flower does not
matter, what matters is flowering
and the flowering is the same.

SLOWING

DOWN

There is infinite time. There is
no end to it, so there is no hurry.
Speak less, think less, do less.
Lessen every activity and you will
be surprised that just by slowing
down the pace of life a great
silence arises. And once you have
tasted it, more becomes available:
you can slow down more.

ADVENTURE

Life is there to be lived. Life has
no question mark; it is a mystery
there is no explanation. And
it is good that there is none: it
would be a great misfortune
if there were an explanation.
If there were an answer that
could satisfy you, just think
how flat things would become,
how boring, how monotonous –
because no answer can answer
your questions. Life remains
an adventure, it remains
a constant search.

POSSIBILITIES

Everybody grows old, but very
few people grow up. Growing up
means you are becoming more
mature every moment, you are
learning, experiencing
everything of life.
This life is a gift. It is a university
to learn, to become aware of all
possibilities, experiences.
Go through them. Don't escape.

EXPERIENCING

The only evidence of life growing
to this stage of consciousness —
of love, of silence, of experiencing
the cosmos — has happened on
this small earth. At any cost,
this earth and the people of this
earth have to be saved from the
calamity that is coming from
your whole past.

PARTICIPATION

Participate in life!
Participate as deeply, as
totally, as possible. Risk all for
participation. If you want to
know what dance is, don't go and
see a dancer — learn dancing,
be a dancer. If you want to know
anything, participate! That is
the true and the right way, the
authentic way, to know
a thing. And there will be
great meaning in your life.
And not only
one-dimensional —
multidimensional meanings.

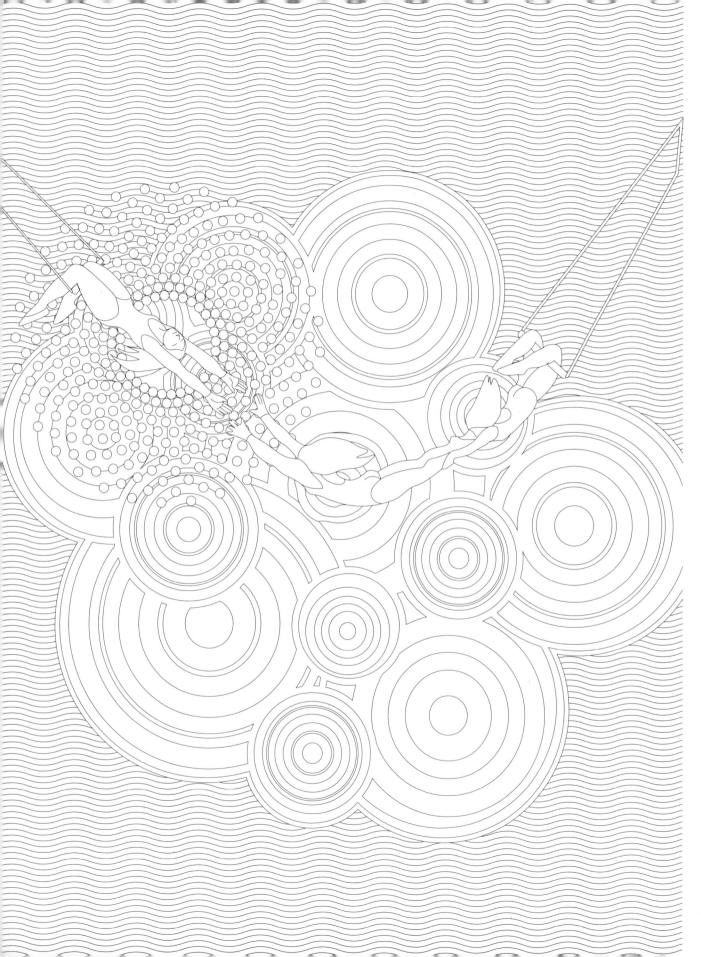

TOTALITY

Live this moment to its totality,
to its very intensity. Perhaps out
of that totality and intensity, you
may get the taste that will go on
lingering with you into the next
moment. And once you have
known that a moment can be
lived with totality and intensity,
you know the secret, the very
secret of life. You are always given
a single moment; you are not
given two moments together.

SUCCESS

Life consists of these polarities: good and bad, success and failure, day and night, summer and winter, birth and death, marriage and divorce, love and hate. The whole life consists of these diametrically opposite polarities — and you are the whole. You cannot choose half of it.

TRAVELING

Life is a pilgrimage. In fact, there is no goal to it. You are always arriving and arriving an[d] arriving, but you never arrive. A[ll] goals are just to keep you movin[g] growing. All goals are like the horizon which seems so close, ju[st] a few miles away. You think yo[u] can reach it, but you cannot ev[er] reach it, because it is only an appearance.

EXHAUSTION

We are living an exhausted life. It is not that we are exhausted just in the evening, in the morning we are also exhausted. What has happened?

Man needs continuous contact with the inner source. So don't ask me how an exhausted man can meditate. It is like asking me how a diseased man, an ill man, can take medicine. He needs it, and only he needs it. You are exhausted — meditation will be a medicine to you.

SUPPRESSION

A person who has lived in jail for many years becomes very afraid when the day that he is going to be free and back in the world comes closer; it frightens him. He will have to earn bread, and he will have to think of a house; he will have a thousand and one worries to face.

That's what happens in inner, psychological prisons too: if you have suppressed for many years, you are afraid. But that fear has to be dropped, and the only way to drop it is to go into situations where you have to drop it...

THE SOURCE

I am against organization. It has
a hierarchy, it moves from the
lowest to the highest in a vertical
line. Organism is a circle, not a
vertical line; no hierarchy, a circle.
Nobody is higher than anybody
else. And the circle has a center
and that center is the source of
energy for all, for all the organs
which make the circle.
Every living thing is an organism.
Every dead thing is
an organization.

FRIENDLINESS

Life is a mirror, it reflects your face. Be friendly, and all of life will reflect friendliness. People know perfectly well that if you are friendly to a dog even the dog becomes friendly to you, so friendly. And there are people who have known that if you are friendly to a tree, the tree becomes friendly to you.

ICE-OLATION

Always remember the difference between isolation and solitude. This is the difference. Isolation is a sort of suppression – forcing yourself to be still, being alone, cutting yourself off from other people. Solitude is not isolation. You are not cutting anything, because there is nothing to cut. You are not trying to be alone; you are simply alone, and there is no effort involved.

THE BURDEN

Have you watched people? – they walk as if they are being weighed down, as though they are carrying a heavy burden on their heads. Drop this burden and say yes to joy! Give a lion's roar of joy! Let the world know that no matter what kind of life you have it can be made into a song, it can be filled with joy. Life can become music

COMPARISON

The whole attitude of comparison is based on the feeling of alikeness. But no one is alike. It is not that one man and another man can be compared — no. They cannot be compared. They are so absolutely different — more different than a tree and a woman. Nothing is alike; every existence is unique. But this uniqueness can only be felt when you don't escape into dreaming. Be with the facts and you will come to know that everyone is unique, not that you are unique. If you feel, "I am unique," you are still in comparison, because this uniqueness is that in comparison to someone else, "I am unique." If someone says, "I am unique," then it is still a comparison. When you feel that everyone is unique, every moment of time, every stone, every tree, every leaf of a tree is unique...

SORROW

If you want to remain superficial, then choose anything, either joy or sorrow, because whatever you choose, you have chosen the other too. Today you may be joyful, tomorrow you will be sorrowful, because life always keeps balance. But it has nothing to do with spiritual growth.
Spiritual growth is going beyond joy and beyond sorrow. In other words, spiritual growth means going beyond all contradictions.

POLITICS

If you want to be intelligent you cannot be in politics. Politics needs idiots, people who can lie, people who can go on lying, people who have double faces, people who can change their personality any moment. They don't have any individuality. If you want to be intelligent you cannot be in any politics.

MOMENT TO MOMENT

Life itself is unpredictable, unmanageable.

Life as such always moves from moment to moment toward the unknown. It is an opening into the unknown — nothing more, nothing less.

If you are open, just like life itself, then you necessarily live in each of your dimensions: the physical, the intellectual, the emotional, the spiritual. Then you live totally; then there is no bifurcation, no division.

POSTPONEMENT

...Never put off until tomorrow what you can enjoy today.... If you enjoy it today, you can enjoy it tomorrow too. Why postpone it? Postponement is a disease of the mind; it always goes on saying, "Tomorrow"... articularly for significant things. Any trivia and rubbish it will do today, the significant can be done tomorrow. But that tomorrow never comes: all that comes is always today. And if you have become accustomed o postponing for tomorrow, you have postponed your life completely.

GUILT

Guilt is a strategy, a strategy to exploit people: make them feel guilty. Once you have succeeded in making them feel guilty, they will be your slaves. Because of the guilt they will never be integrated enough, because of the guilt they will remain divided. Because of the guilt they will never be able to accept themselves, they will be always condemning. Because of the guilt they will be ready to believe in anything. Just to get rid of guilt they will do anything. Any nonsense, any nonsense ritual they will perform just to get rid of the guilt.

REBIRTH

Miss the present and you live in boredom. Be in the present and you will be surprised that there is no boredom at all. Start by looking around a little more like a child. Be a child again! That's what meditation is all about — being a child again — a rebirth , being innocent again, not-knowing.

CONSCIOUSNESS

Man lives in misery – not
because he is destined to live
in misery but because he does
not understand his own nature,
potential, possibilities of growth.
This non-understanding
of oneself creates hell. To
understand oneself is to be
naturally blissful, because bliss
is not something that comes
from the outside, it is your
consciousness resting in its
own nature.
Remember this statement: your
consciousness resting in itself is
what bliss is all about.

GUIDANCE

Nobody needs personal guidance, because all personal guidance is a beautiful name for dependence on somebody and he is going to distort you...you should become silent, so that you can listen to your still, small voice. That is your real guide; the guide is within you.

THE MISER

Don't try to possess anything. At the most use, and be thankful that you were allowed to use, but don't possess.
Possession is a miserliness; and a miserly being cannot flower. A miserly being is always in a spiritual constipation, ill.
You have to open, share. Share whatsoever you have and it will grow — share more and it grows more. Go on giving, and you are continuously refilled. The source is eternal; don't be a miser. And whatsoever it is — love, wisdom — whatsoever it is, share.

THE
OUTSIDER

It is always love that heals, because love makes you whole, love makes you feel welcome in the world, love makes you a part of existence. It destroys alienation. Then you are no more an outsider here, but utterly needed. Love makes you feel needed, and to be needed is the greatest need. Nothing else can fulfill that great need. Unless you feel that you are contributing something to existence, unless you feel that without you the existence would be a little less, that you would be missed, that you are irreplaceable, you will not feel healthy and whole.

COMPROMISE

One compromises because one
is not certain about one's truth,
one is not certain about one's
own experience. The moment
you have experienced something
it is impossible to compromise.
There is no possibility at all.
You compromise only because
your idea is only a mind thing,
a borrowed thought. You don't
know whether it is right or
wrong, so even if half proves to b
right, it is not a bad bargain...
Compromise simply means
you are on uncertain ground.
Rather than compromising, find
grounding, roots, individuality.
Find a sincerity of feeling, the
support of your heart. Then
whatever the consequence, it doe
not matter.

PATIENCE

Women can wait, and they can wait infinitely, their patience is infinite. It has to be so, because a child has to be carried for nine months. Every day it becomes heavier and heavier and heavier, and more and more difficult. You have to be patient and wait, and nothing can be done about it. You even have to love your burden, and wait and dream that the child will be born. And look at a mother, a woman who is just about to be a mother: she becomes more beautiful, because when she waits she flowers.

ORDINARINESS

Everybody wants to be
extraordinary, that is very
ordinary. But to be ordinary
and just relax in being
ordinary, that is superbly
extraordinary. One who can
accept one's ordinariness without
any grudge, any grumbling —
with joy, because this is how the
whole existence is — then nobody
can destroy your bliss.
Nobody can steal it, nobody can
take it away. Then wherever you
are, you will be in bliss.
To me, the ordinary is the most
extraordinary phenomenon
in existence.

RIPENESS

Everything happens only in its own time. Ripeness is all; just don't be in a hurry; the fruit is ripening every day. The moment is coming closer and closer when suddenly, without any previous notice, the fruit falls from the tree.

WE ARE
THE WORLD

If we can fill the world with a few million meditators, lovers, rejoicing and dancing and celebrating, humanity can yet be saved. There is still a chance, all hope is not lost.

MATURITY

Maturity is a rebirth, a spiritual birth. You are born anew, you are a child again. With fresh eyes you start looking at existence. With love in the heart you approach life. With silence and innocence you penetrate your own innermost core. You are no more just the head. Now you use the head, but it is your servant. First you become the heart, and then you transcend even the heart....

Going beyond thoughts and feelings and becoming a pure ness is maturity. Maturity is the ultimate flowering of meditation.

TURNING IN

You don't have to wander around the world. Just a small turning in is enough, and all that you have longed for, for lives, is suddenly revealed to be your own self. You were searching for yourself, and that was your suffering: you could not find yourself.

You could not find yourself in riches, or in power; you could not find your so-called love. You have looked everywhere, you have walked thousands of ways in thousands of lives, but you have never reached to yourself. This is the basic suffering: not to know yourself. Not to be aware of your eternity is the only misery — all miseries are small expressions of it.

CLINGING TO THE PAST

One thing has to be remembered, that the past is no more, and clinging to the past is clinging to the dead. It is very dangerous, because it hampers and hinders your life, in the present and for the future. One should always go on freeing himself of the dead past.

THE DREAM

We are alone, all togetherness
is just a dream, because in fact
there are not two to be together:
only one exists. So all relationship
is illusory. There is nobody to
relate to — only consciousness
exists...

That is the ultimate peak of
understanding. With that
understanding, all misery
disappears. The misery is created
by the illusion of the other.

PROJECTION

*All the seekers of human
consciousness absolutely agree
on the point that all your misery
or your happiness, your sadness
or your joy, is nothing but your
projection. It is coming deep from
your unconscious mind and the
other person is functioning only
like a screen. Once it is fulfilled,
you are finished. And suddenly,
the same woman you were
ready to die for...you are ready
to kill her.
Strange...such a great change.
Love turns into hate so easily.
And yet you are not aware that
love and hate both are
your projections.*

LETTING GO

All fear, all is the same. You are afraid of going into something more powerful than you because a dewdrop dropping into the ocean is bound to disappear; it is death to the dewdrop. The more powerful will absorb you; hence, the fear.
But if you know that your life is the greatest power in existence, there is nothing more powerful than it, not even nuclear weapons can absorb it...once you become certain about it, then the dewdrop knows it is not his disappearance in the ocean, it is the ocean disappearing in the dewdrop. It is the dewdrop becoming as vast as the ocean.
It is not disappearance; it is becoming infinite, unbounded.

LAZINESS

Laziness and easiness look so alike that it is very easy to misunderstand which is which.

If you are enjoying your aloneness, it cannot be laziness because laziness always feels a certain guilt, a certain feeling that "I am doing something that should not be doing," that "I am not participating in existence."

Laziness means you have dropped out of the creativity of the universe — you are standing aside while the universe goes on creating day in, day out.

HARMONY

Existence is harmony, it is not anarchy. It is not a chaos, it is a cosmos. It is a unity: so complex so vast, but still united. And life pulsates – from the lowest atom to the highest star. Wavelengths differ, pulsations are of different frequencies, but the whole pulsates in a deep unity, in a harmony.

GOING WITH
THE FLOW

Thinking yourself separate from existence is the ego. Thinking yourself one with existence is trust.
Don't protect yourself. Protection means you have believed the false idea that you are separate. Don't push the river. Go with the flow of existence. ...
Waking, wake. Sleeping, sleep. Let there be no separation between you and the life that surrounds you.

SCHIZOPHRENIA

Beyond your intellect is your feeling. Another name for your feeling is intuition, a more scientific name. But very few people reach to intuition, because to reach to intuition, you have to go beyond intellect, and meditation is the only way. But unfortunately meditation is not part of our education. Education stops at intellect, creating a quarrel between your instinct and intellect, creating a split, a schizophrenia that you will suffer from your whole life. If you meditate, something beyond intellect starts functioning. You can call it the heart, you can call it intuition. It has no arguments, but it has tremendous experiences.

STRESS

Stress comes when one is result-oriented. You will not get anything out of it; you are doing it out of the sheer joy of doing it. Stress is irrelevant. Stress is natural when you are looking for some result. Then the result is heavy on the head...Stress comes always out of the goal. When there is no goal there is no stress. It is more like a morning walk than going anywhere. You can enjoy the sun and the birds and the trees and the people on the road. And you can turn back from anywhere because you were not going anywhere; there was no target.

SHARING

If you have something, somethi[n]
that gives you joy, peace, ecstas[y]
share it. And remember that
when you share there is no
motive. I am not saying that
by sharing it you will reach to
heaven. I am not giving you
any goal. I am saying to you,
just by sharing it you will be
tremendously fulfilled. In the ve[ry]
sharing is the fulfillment, there [is]
no goal beyond it. It is not end[-]
oriented, it is an end unto itsel[f.]

NO-THINGNESS

The Western mind associates zero with nothingness. The Eastern understanding of the zero is not of nothingness but of no-thingness — and there is a vast difference between the two. Nothingness gives you a negative idea; no-thingness gives you the idea of space. There is no thing in it but there is spaciousness. It is full, full of space ...

We are so full of rubbish, junk, garbage — all kinds of furniture.

All our thoughts, desires, memories, imagination, fantasies, are nothing but rotten furniture. We have to throw it out so that space can be created. Once you are full of space and nothing else, the miracle happens: the whole universe rushes into you, Then the stars are within you and the flowers are within you and the birds are singing within you. Then suddenly you are in a deep harmony with the whole, you are the whole. And to me that's the only possibility of being holy: to become one with the whole.

ABOUT OSHO

Osho's unique contribution to the understanding of who we are defies categorization. Mystic and scientist, a rebellious spirit whose sole interest is to alert humanity to the urgent need to discover a new way of living. To continue as before is to invite threats to our very survival on this unique and beautiful planet.

His essential point is that only by changing ourselves, one individual at a time, can the outcome of all our "selves" — our societies, our cultures, our beliefs, our world — also change. The doorway to that change is meditation.

Osho the scientist has experimented and scrutinized all the approaches of the past and examined their effects on the modern human being and responded to their shortcomings by creating a new starting point for the hyperactive 21st Century mind: OSHO Active Meditations.

Once the agitation of a modern lifetime has started to settle, "activity" can melt into "passivity," a key starting point of real meditation. To support this next step, Osho has transformed the ancient "art of listening" into a subtle contemporary methodology: the OSHO Talks. Here words become music, the listener discovers who is listening, and the awareness moves from what is being heard to the individual doing the listening. Magically, as silence arises, what needs to be heard is understood directly, free from the distraction of a mind that can only interrupt and interfere with this delicate process.

These thousands of talks cover everything from the individual quest for meaning to the most urgent social and political issues facing society today. Osho's books are not written but are transcribed from audio and video recordings of these extemporaneous talks to international audiences. As he puts it, "So remember: whatever I am saying is not just for you...I am talking also for the future generations."

Osho has been described by *The Sunday Times* in London as one of the "1000 Makers of the 20th Century" and by American author Tom Robbins as "the most dangerous man since Jesus Christ." *Sunday Mid-Day* (India) has selected Osho as one of ten people — along with Gandhi, Nehru and Buddha — who have changed the destiny of India.

About his own work Osho has said that he is helping to create the conditions for the birth of a new kind of human being. He often characterizes this new human being as "Zorba the Buddha" — capable both of enjoying the earthy pleasures of a Zorba the Greek and the silent serenity of a Gautama the Buddha.

Running like a thread through all aspects of Osho's talks and meditations is a vision that encompasses both the timeless wisdom of all ages past and the highest potential of today's (and tomorrow's) science and technology.

Osho is known for his revolutionary contribution to the science of inner transformation, with an approach to meditation that acknowledges the accelerated pace of contemporary life. His unique OSHO Active Meditations™ are designed to first release the accumulated stresses of body and mind, so that it is then easier to take an experience of stillness and thought-free relaxation into daily life.

Two autobiographical works by the author are available:
Autobiography of a Spiritually Incorrect Mystic,
St Martins Press, New York (book and eBook)
Glimpses of a Golden Childhood,
OSHO Media International, Pune, India (book and eBook)